CATS

SEYMOUR SIMON

CATS

SCHOLASTIC INC.
New York Toronto London Auckland Sydney
Mexico City New Delhi Hong Kong Buenos Aires

To Joyce and the feral cats who became our pets:

Mittens and Sir Isaac Newton (Newty Frewty)

Special thanks to Dan Wharton, Director, Central Park Zoo,

Wildlife Conservation Society, for his expert advice.

All cats are hunting animals. They use claws and teeth to seize their prey. When you watch a cat play with a ball or a piece of yarn, it is almost like watching a tiger or a leopard stalking its prey in the wild. Even well-fed pet cats will try to catch mice or birds or insects.

Cats are great fun to watch. They make good pets, but they do not act at all like dogs. Dogs are noisy, friendly, and lively. Cats are quiet. They may disappear for hours without your being able to find them. But cats can also be friendly and will sit on your lap purring contentedly while you stroke their fur. Learning about cats can help you select your pet cat and take better care of it.

About five thousand years ago, wild cats were first tamed in ancient Egypt. They were used to protect stored grain from mice and other rodents. Early Egyptians considered cats sacred animals. When a cat died, there was a period of mourning. Then the cat was mummified and buried in a casket in a cat cemetery. In one ancient Egyptian cat cemetery, more than 300,000 cat mummies were found.

From Egypt, pet cats began to spread across Asia and Europe. In Siam (Thailand today), only the king and the royal family owned cats. The Siamese cat was the royal cat of Siam. By the Middle Ages, cats had become very popular in France and England. In the 1600s, they came to the Americas with the colonists. Nowadays, pet cats live with people in countries around the world.

Cats are not very big. Adults usually weigh between six and fifteen pounds. Cats have slim and flexible bodies. They can twist their bodies in amazing ways. The bones in a cat's back are much more loosely connected than the bones in your back. This makes a cat's body very bendable.

Cats are great climbers and jumpers. They also use their tails for balance. When a cat jumps, its body uncoils like a spring. A cat absorbs the landing shock easily with its front legs and the cushioning pads on its front paws. When a cat falls several feet, it twists its body in midair and lands on all fours, usually without hurting itself. This may be why people sometimes say a cat has nine lives.

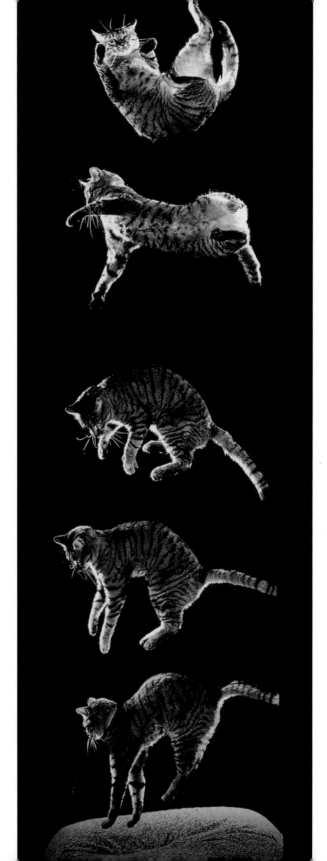

Some people think that cats can see in the dark. Cats have excellent vision, but even they can't see in total darkness. They *can* see in light that is only one sixth as bright as the light humans need for seeing.

Cats have a special mirrorlike surface in the back of the eye called the *tapetum*. Faint light passes through the eye and then is reflected by the tapetum back out of the eye. The reflected light is what makes cats' eyes gleam in the dark and helps them see better at night.

Cats can see in color, but it doesn't mean much to an animal that hunts at night. Color plays no part in hunting a mouse in dim light or deciding to nuzzle against your red shirt rather than your blue one.

Cats also have a good sense of hearing. They can hear sounds that are too soft or too high-pitched for humans to hear. A cat turns its ears very quickly to locate the direction of a sound. Hearing helps cats hunt for mice and other little animals when they move about.

A cat's whiskers are very sensitive to touch. Cats have whiskers on the chin, over the eyes, and on the backs of the front legs—not just on the upper lip. In the dark, whiskers help a cat sense objects that it cannot see. But it is not true that a cat's facial whiskers are exactly equal to the width of the cat's body.

Smell is another important sense in cats. Cats often will not eat food that has turned stale because of its bad odor. Cats have about nineteen million "smelling" nerve endings in their noses. Humans have only about five million. Cats love the smell of a plant called catnip. They sometimes roll around in catnip making happy sounds.

Cats are fussy eaters. Dogs will eat almost anything you give them off the table, but cats are much pickier. They don't have a "sweet tooth" and won't eat cookies or candy bars the way that dogs will.

If you have a pet cat, you may have tried to train it not to scratch the furniture. You may even have tried to teach your cat not to bring a dead mouse into the house. But a cat doesn't seem to learn these simple household rules. Does that mean that a cat is stupid or has a poor memory?

Neither is true. Cats learn and remember those things that are useful to them, but not necessarily useful to you. It quickly remembers the location of the food and water dishes and the litter box. A cat even seems to remember its own name at mealtimes when it is called.

Cats remember things in their neighborhoods they want to avoid, like a pesky dog. They may even remember where they live if taken away from home. But only with skillful training will a cat remember what YOU want it to remember.

Cats can't talk by using words the way people do. But cats make sounds that tell you or other cats how they're feeling or what they want. Cats purr, gurgle, meow, wail, hiss, screech, and growl. Each of these sounds means something different.

Purring usually means everything is fine. Kittens purr to their mothers and mothers purr to their kittens. Adult cats purr to each other when they are peaceful. Cats purr when you

pet them. Gurgling is another happy sound cats make. Sometimes a cat will gurgle and meow for minutes in a kind of a "cat chat" with another cat.

A kitten meows if it is cold or lost or wants to be fed. Adult cats meow if they're hungry or unhappy about something. Hissing, screeching, and growling are angry sounds. The awful screech a tomcat makes at night is a cry of warning to other tomcats in the area to keep away from a female cat.

Cats also use body language to show what they're feeling. When a cat rubs itself against your legs or against another cat, it is happy and affectionate. If a cat points its ears forward, it signals friendly interest and watchfulness. An angry cat raises its ears and points them backward, narrows its eyes to slits, and pushes its whiskers forward. A cat that is hunting or playing opens its eyes wide, perks up its ears, and bristles its whiskers. When a cat is petted and happy, it partly closes its eyes and relaxes its body and whiskers.

When a cat arches its back, flattens its ears, and shows its teeth, the cat is afraid and defensive. If a cat is frightened, its hair stands up all over and its tail goes down. If it's about to pounce or attack, its hair stands up along the spine and tail. The tail whips from side to side or suddenly stands up.

There are many different ways that a cat "talks." Watch your cat carefully and you'll soon be able to figure out what each sound and body movement means.

By the time they are a year old, female cats can have babies. After mating with a male cat, a mother cat will give birth to a litter of kittens in about 65 days. A litter can contain as many as a dozen kittens. The average litter is four kittens.

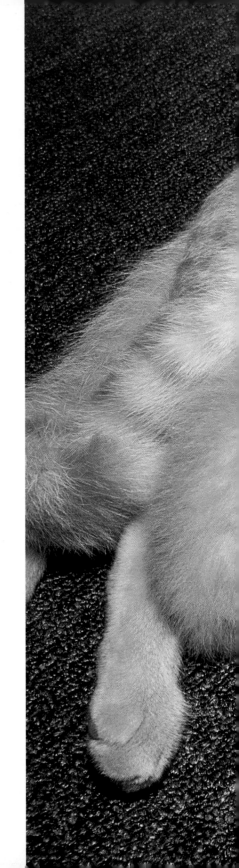

Kittens usually are born from five minutes to two hours apart. A kitten is born in a cloudy white sac filled with fluid. The mother licks each newborn kitten, breaks the sac, and removes the fluid from its face. Licking makes the kitten start to breathe.

The mother also bites through the *umbilicus* (the cord that carried food to the fetus and took away its waste while it was inside the mother). Even a first-time mother cat seems to know exactly what to do.

Right away, the newborn kittens suckle milk from their mother. She purrs and nuzzles them as they feed.

A newborn kitten is mostly helpless. Its eyelids are closed. Its ears are laid back. The tiny kitten can't see or hear. It weighs only two to five ounces. It's only about as long as a pencil. At birth, a kitten can wriggle and squirm, but it cannot walk.

Newborns snuggle together for the first week or so. The mother licks her kittens often. She carries them gently but firmly by the scruff of the neck. The mother and the babies soon learn to recognize each other by smell.

About eight days after birth, a kitten begins to open its eyes. In less than three weeks, it can see and hear.

A one-month-old kitten runs around and plays. It can weigh between nine ounces and eighteen ounces, which is just over one pound. By the end of its second month, a kitten eats solid food and has stopped nursing. A four-month-old kitten is completely independent of its mother.

Over the last century, people have developed more than one hundred different varieties of cats, called breeds. A cat can be a purebred or mixed-breed cat. Purebred cats are usually divided into two groups: longhaired cats and shorthaired cats.

The most popular breed of longhaired cat is called a Persian or simply a longhair. A Persian's fur is soft and may grow as long as five inches. It has a sturdy body, a round face, a short nose, round eyes, and short legs. A Persian's fur can be black, white, red, blue, smoky, tortoiseshell, calico, pewter, chocolate, or other color combinations.

Persians are usually quiet, even-tempered cats. That makes them ideal pets for people who keep their cats indoors.

Other longhaired cats, such as the Angora or the Balinese cat, have slimmer bodies and are more active than Persians. They are gentle, friendly, and playful.

A feral cat is a house cat that has gone back to being wild. For a feral cat living in a city or a big cat in the wild, having short hair can be an advantage. That's because long hair can get tangled on things when a cat is stalking its prey. Long hair also gives a cat's enemy something to grab on to. Shorthaired cats are far more common in nature than longhaired ones.

There are many kinds of purebred shorthaired cats, including British shorthairs, American shorthairs, Siamese, Manxes, and Abyssinians. The Siamese is a slender cat with blue eyes and a really loud "meow." The Manx is a tailless breed. The Abyssinian looks like the cat that ancient Egyptians worshipped.

Whether your cat is a purebred longhaired or shorthaired cat or a mixed-breed cat, it can make a good family pet.

Here are some questions you and your family may want to think about before you decide to get a pet cat.

- Do you have enough room for a cat's food dish, water dish, and litter box?
- Will your cat have to be indoors all the time, or can it be allowed outdoors? Remember, all kinds of cats prey on birds. Consider putting a collar with a bell on your pet cat if you allow it to go outdoors.
- Will you or other family members have the time and patience to care for a cat regularly?
- Can your family make arrangements to take care of the cat if you go away for many days on a trip?

You also have to think about what kind of cat you want. Should you get a purebred or a mixed-breed cat? If you'd like a purebred cat, what kind do you want? Do you want a male or a female cat? Do you want a kitten or an adult? Should you adopt a cat from an animal shelter or from a friend or buy one from a cat breeder? You and your family need to find out as much as you can about having a pet cat before making these decisions.

For many people, cats make ideal pets. Watching a cat is never dull. A cat loves to explore. It will play with a string or stalk an object. It will climb almost anything and get into the most unlikely places. It can be quiet or friendly with its owner. Cats are wonderful and mysterious animals. Just ask anyone who has ever owned a cat!